Embrace the end
Enrich the moment
Glimpse the eternal

The Truth About Death

Mortality Unveiled

QUESTIONS & ANSWERS

TALAL ITANI

The Truth About Death: Mortality Unveiled

Copyright © 2025 by Talal Itani

No part of this book may be reproduced, stored, or transmitted by any means without prior written permission from the author, except as permitted by copyright law. Brief quotations are allowed for review or commentary if the source is credited.

First Edition: January 2025
ISBN: 978-0-9861368-9-4

Published by Diff Books
Plano, Texas, USA

To contact the author: me@talal-i.com

This book is intended for informational and spiritual reflection purposes only. It is not a substitute for professional medical, legal, or mental health advice. If you are in crisis or experiencing ongoing distress, please consult a qualified professional. The author and publisher disclaim responsibility for any actions taken based on the content of this book.

What's Inside:

Understanding the Nature of Death 1
Why do we die? 2
Is death the end or a transition? 3
If we all die, what's the purpose of life? 4
Why is death part of life's design? 5

The Soul, the Body, and the Afterlife 7
What happens to our soul when we die? 8
What happens to our body when we die? 9
Does the soul wait between death and the afterlife? 10
What if someone believes in reincarnation? 11
Does it matter if I'm buried or cremated? 12
Is it okay to donate my body to science? 13
Is it okay to donate my organs for transplant? 14

Facing Mortality: Fears and Uncertainties 15
Can a person escape death? 17
What does it mean to conquer death? 18
Is dying painful? 19
What makes us fear death? 20
Is it normal to fear dying more than death itself? 21
Why does death feel unfair sometimes? 22
Why do some desperately seek reasons for tragic death? . 23
Does embracing mortality ease anxiety, bring happiness? 24

How does reflecting on death spur personal growth?.......25

Does mortality give life more meaning?..............................26

Why is death a difficult topic to discuss?...........................27

Are we all truly equal in death?..28

Are animals aware of mortality?..29

The Afterlife and Belief **31**

Can we know what happens after death?............................32

Do we all go to heaven?..33

What if I worry my sins won't be forgiven before I die?..34

What if someone doesn't believe in an afterlife?...............35

Will we be reunited with loved ones after death?.............36

Is there a chance for learning or growth in the afterlife?..37

Is eternal life endless bliss or endless suffering?................38

Contact with the Deceased: Myths and Realities..........**39**

Does a deceased person see or hear us?...............................40

Can the deceased help or influence events in this life?.....41

Can a deceased person intercede for me?...........................42

Is it permissible to pray to the deceased?............................43

Do spirits or 'energies' linger in familiar places?...............44

Is it okay to think about someone who died?.....................45

Can I keep a relationship with someone who died?..........46

Do dreams about the deceased mean anything?................47

Grief and Emotional Responses..**49**

Why do we grieve after someone dies?................................51

Is it normal to cry or feel numb after a loss? 52

What if I don't cry or feel sad after losing someone? 53

How do I cope with the death of a loved one? 54

How can I handle guilt after losing a loved one? 55

Is it wrong to feel happy after losing someone? 56

Why do we feel anger after a loss? 57

What are the stages of grief? Are they universal? 58

Is my grief normal, or is it depression or mental illness? .. 59

How can I heal after parting on bad terms? 60

Does time heal all wounds? Does grief last forever? 61

Why do some people avoid grieving? 62

Why are some at peace with death, and others not? 63

Can someone's death bring relief to those left behind? 64

How and why do relationships change after a death? 65

Faith, Doubt, and Spiritual Perspectives 67

Does faith change our perception of death? 68

Is it normal to question my faith after a major loss? 69

Is anger toward the Creator normal after a major loss? 70

Do all religions view death the same way? 71

Is the angel of death real? 72

What do near-death experiences teach us? 73

Complex End-of-Life Questions 75

Is it natural to wish for death during hard times? 76

Is it ever justifiable to end one's own life? 77

What is euthanasia, and why is it controversial?...............78
Should we use all medical means to prolong life?..............79
Can someone return to life after dying?..........................80
Can someone bring the dead back to life?........................81

Overcoming Fear and Living Fully..83
How can I stop worrying about death?..............................84
How do I find peace with death?..85
How can I live fully knowing I will die?............................86

Children and Death..87
Why do some people die young?...88
How do children see death differently than adults?..........89
How do I help a child understand death?..........................90
How do I help a child cope with losing a loved one?........91

Supporting Others Through Death....................................93
How can I comfort someone who is grieving?..................94
How can I support someone who is dying?......................95

Preparing for Our Own End..97
How do I settle unresolved conflicts before I die?............98
How do I ensure my dependents' care after I'm gone?......99
What does it mean to embrace mortality?........................100
Does the world change when we die?...............................101
What do we leave behind after we die?............................102
How should we die?..103

Chapter 1

Understanding the Nature of Death

Questions answered in this chapter:

Why do we die?

Is death the end or a transition?

If we all die, what's the purpose of life?

Why is death part of life's design?

Chapter 1 - Understanding the Nature of Death

Why do we die?

We die because mortality is a fundamental part of existence. It's not a flaw or accident, but an intentional aspect of life's design. All living things—microorganisms, plants, animals, and humans—are biologically programmed to age, decay, and eventually die. This process is ingrained in the design of all life on Earth, ensuring that existence follows a natural order.

Beyond its biological reality, death reminds us of life's impermanence, urging us to reflect on its deeper purpose. By embracing mortality, we can discover meaning in our existence and cherish the fleeting beauty of every moment.

Chapter 1 - Understanding the Nature of Death

Is death the end or a transition?

Death is not the end—it is a transition into the next phase of existence. It marks the closure of our earthly life and the beginning of the eternal journey that awaits. While it's natural to view death as final, it is, in truth, a doorway to the hereafter, where the outcomes of our earthly actions are revealed, and divine justice is fulfilled.

Regardless of how we view death, it remains a passage that leads us to a greater reality shaped by divine purpose and justice. By seeing it this way, we shift our perspective from death as a final ending to a meaningful transition into what lies beyond.

Chapter 1 - Understanding the Nature of Death

If we all die, what's the purpose of life?

Life is a journey with a clear beginning and end, and we are travelers passing through this temporary world. Our time here is brief, like that of a visitor exploring a land that is not his permanent home.

The purpose of life is to be tested—to make choices that reflect truth, goodness, and righteousness. Above all, we are here to know and serve the Creator, fulfilling the purpose for which we were created and preparing for the eternal life that follows.

Chapter 1 - Understanding the Nature of Death

Why is death part of life's design?

Death is part of life's design because it is the will of the Creator, woven into the very nature of existence for every living being—humans, animals, plants, and even the smallest microorganisms. The fact that all life eventually comes to an end underscores our limited time on Earth, reminding us that this world is not our permanent home.

Recognizing the certainty of death can also serve as a powerful source of inspiration. It motivates us to live with greater intention, strengthen our relationships, and focus on what truly matters. Through this reflection on life's fleeting nature, we nurture gratitude and purpose, preparing ourselves for the destiny that awaits us beyond this temporary realm.

CHAPTER 2

The Soul, the Body, and the Afterlife

Questions answered in this chapter:

What happens to our soul when we die?

What happens to our body when we die?

Does the soul wait between death and the afterlife?

What if someone believes in reincarnation?

Does it matter if I'm buried or cremated?

Is it okay to donate my body to science?

Is it okay to donate my organs for transplant?

Chapter 2 - The Soul, the Body, and the Afterlife

What happens to our soul when we die?

When we die, our soul leaves the physical world and enters a spiritual realm, free from the confines of the body. This marks the start of a new phase of existence—a reality beyond earthly limits, where the soul's true nature is fully revealed.

Following this transition, we encounter divine judgment—a moment of perfect justice in which every action, intention, and choice is taken into account. Nothing is overlooked, and all our deeds are weighed with absolute fairness. In keeping with this justice, those who have lived righteously experience eternal bliss and fulfillment, while those who have done wrong face just consequences. Through this process, each soul receives the outcome it has earned, as it continues onward in the eternal journey.

Chapter 2 - The Soul, the Body, and the Afterlife

What happens to our body when we die?

After death, the body naturally begins to decompose. Cells break down, and bacteria—both within and around the body—initiate decay. Over time, tissues disintegrate, returning the physical remains to the earth. This process reflects the broader cycle of life, where all living things eventually pass on and nourish future existence.

Beyond these biological changes, cultural and religious practices guide how the body is laid to rest. Traditions such as burial, cremation, or other rites show collective reverence for the deceased and acknowledge the finality of the physical life.

Chapter 2 - The Soul, the Body, and the Afterlife

Does the soul wait between death and the afterlife?

Yes. After the body's death, the soul enters an interim phase, existing in a realm separate from earthly life but not yet at its final destination. During this time, the soul remains aware and awaits the Day of Resurrection, when it will face ultimate judgment. Although the exact nature of this waiting period is beyond human understanding, one thing is clear: life does not simply end at death. The soul continues in a conscious state until the appointed time of resurrection.

Eventually, on that Day of Resurrection, every soul will be called to account. Until then, the soul remains in this in-between realm, reminding us to live responsibly now and prepare spiritually before our time here concludes.

Chapter 2 - The Soul, the Body, and the Afterlife

What if someone believes in reincarnation?

Different faiths and philosophies offer various teachings about what happens after death. While this book presents the view of a single earthly life leading to an eternal hereafter, others believe in a cycle of rebirth. Although these perspectives differ, most traditions emphasize that our actions have lasting consequences.

Ultimately, whether one envisions a final judgment or repeated lifetimes, the underlying message is similar: live ethically and strive for a higher purpose. By focusing on goodness, compassion, and spiritual growth, we create a life that resonates with the values of our chosen path—regardless of how we believe it continues beyond this world.

Chapter 2 - The Soul, the Body, and the Afterlife

Does it matter if I'm buried or cremated?

It does not matter in terms of your fate. While faiths and cultures have their own burial or cremation traditions—primarily to honor the deceased and help the living find closure—your afterlife depends on the state of your soul and the life you led, not on the manner of your burial. The Creator's judgment is rooted in His perfect knowledge of your intentions, actions, and relationship with Him, rather than any specific funeral rite.

A common concern is whether cremation might prevent resurrection. Yet, the body naturally disintegrates into dust over time, regardless of how it is laid to rest. The Creator, being all-powerful, is fully capable of resurrecting us from any state, ensuring that no physical process can stand in the way of His plan.

Chapter 2 - The Soul, the Body, and the Afterlife

Is it okay to donate my body to science?

Yes. Donating your body to science can greatly benefit medical research and education, potentially improving countless lives. While some traditions or cultures prefer standard burial practices, many faiths and ethical frameworks permit this act of service—provided it is done with respect and sincerity.

What truly matters is the life you lived, the sincerity of your deeds, and your relationship with the Creator. Your decision about your remains does not affect your soul's fate. If you believe donating your body serves the common good, it can be a meaningful final gesture of generosity, reflecting the values you upheld during your lifetime.

Chapter 2 - The Soul, the Body, and the Afterlife

Is it okay to donate my organs for transplant?

Yes. Many moral, religious, and ethical perspectives support organ donation as an act of compassion and service to others. By giving organs that can save or improve lives, you extend kindness and fulfill the principle of helping those in need.

Like full-body donation, organ donation does not affect your ultimate fate in the afterlife. The Creator values sincerity of intention, and donating organs with the goal of saving lives or alleviating suffering can be a powerful final gesture of generosity. If you choose this path, be sure to register your wishes officially and inform your loved ones to avoid any confusion.

CHAPTER 3
Facing Mortality: Fears and Uncertainties

Questions answered in this chapter:

Can a person escape death?

What does it mean to conquer death?

Is dying painful?

What makes us fear death?

Is it normal to fear dying more than death itself?

Why does death feel unfair sometimes?

Why do some desperately seek reasons for tragic death?

Does embracing mortality ease anxiety, bring happiness?

How does reflecting on death spur personal growth?

Does mortality give life more meaning?

Why is death a difficult topic to discuss?

Chapter 2 - The Soul, the Body, and the Afterlife

Are we all truly equal in death?

Are animals aware of mortality?

Chapter 3 - Facing Mortality: Fears and Uncertainties

Can a person escape death?

No. Death is unavoidable and part of life's design. No matter how much we strive to delay or avoid it, every soul will face death at its appointed time. This fundamental truth transcends age, status, and circumstance, reminding us that our earthly existence is finite.

Rather than fearing this certainty, we can view it as a powerful catalyst to live meaningfully. Awareness of our mortality prompts us to cherish our time, invest in our relationships, and uphold our core values. Death unites us all in a shared destiny, urging us to fulfill our purpose in the span of life granted to us.

Chapter 3 - Facing Mortality: Fears and Uncertainties

What does it mean to conquer death?

Conquering death does not mean avoiding or escaping it, but rather accepting it with courage and understanding. When we see mortality as a natural part of life instead of something to dread, we free ourselves to live with greater purpose and integrity. By recognizing that every moment is precious, we commit to meaningful pursuits and deeper connections.

True victory over death emerges when we find peace with its reality and trust in what lies beyond. Death is already a passage to another stage of existence; recognizing this truth can shift our perspective from dread to acceptance. In doing so, we stop trying to "defeat" death and instead focus on living in a way that transcends its power to instill fear.

Chapter 3 - Facing Mortality: Fears and Uncertainties

Is dying painful?

The experience differs from one individual to another. Some may endure physical discomfort or emotional distress, especially in cases of severe illness or sudden trauma. Others find their final moments comparatively peaceful, with minimal suffering. Factors such as one's health, the nature of the illness, and the circumstances of death all influence the degree of pain.

Beyond any physical agony, there can be significant psychological pain tied to confronting the reality of one's life ending. However, believing in an eternal afterlife can help ease this emotional burden. Trusting in a life beyond death offers hope and comfort, reminding us that physical existence, though precious, is not our final home. Ultimately, the process of dying is shaped by both bodily factors and spiritual convictions, making each person's dying experience uniquely their own.

Chapter 3 - Facing Mortality: Fears and Uncertainties

What makes us fear death?

Fear of death often arises from uncertainty about what lies beyond. Facing the end of our earthly existence can feel overwhelming, especially if we're unsure of the afterlife or any continuation of the soul. This fear may also reflect a sense of accountability as we consider how we have lived and what consequences may follow. Leaving behind loved ones and the comforts of the familiar adds an emotional weight that can intensify our apprehension.

Yet, much of this fear can be eased with understanding and preparation. Deepening our faith, exploring life's deeper questions, or practicing self-reflection can bring clarity and reduce the dread of the unknown. When we live mindfully, practice gratitude, and accept our limited time, our view of death shifts from fear to acceptance, letting us see it as a natural step on our path.

Chapter 3 - Facing Mortality: Fears and Uncertainties

Is it normal to fear dying more than death itself?

Yes. Many people find the decline in health, independence, or comfort more unsettling than the notion of being dead. Pain, uncertainty, and a loss of control can feel far more daunting than the abstract idea of nonexistence.

Still, it can help to remember that every living being eventually dies. Finding reassurance in the Creator's plan or sharing your concerns with supportive loved ones can soften these fears. Recognizing our shared fate transforms what seems overwhelming into a journey of compassion and calm.

Chapter 3 - Facing Mortality: Fears and Uncertainties

Why does death feel unfair sometimes?

Death can feel unfair when it arrives unexpectedly or cuts short a life we longed to share. Because we form deep bonds with loved ones, losing them can bring intense pain and a sense that they've been taken too soon. Anger, confusion, and sorrow are natural responses in the face of such a profound loss.

At the same time, acknowledging that death is a universal part of existence can bring perspective. For many, trust in a larger plan—one that sees meaning even in shorter lives—softens the sting of grief. Ultimately, the perception of unfairness reflects our deep love and the significance of the connections we build in life.

Chapter 3 - Facing Mortality: Fears and Uncertainties

Why do some desperately seek reasons for tragic death?

Tragedy often leaves us feeling helpless and overwhelmed. Searching for a reason can help restore a sense of control and make the loss seem less random. By finding an explanation—even if it's incomplete—people hope to ease their pain by understanding how and why it happened.

At the same time, our mortal limits mean we cannot fully grasp every aspect of life's design. The deeper "why" often remains elusive, reminding us that some events lie beyond our control or understanding. Accepting our finiteness can bring a measure of peace, even without a clear explanation. Ultimately, faith and compassion can guide us through uncertainty, helping us to live with both sorrow and hope.

Chapter 3 - Facing Mortality: Fears and Uncertainties

Does embracing mortality ease anxiety, bring happiness?

Yes. Accepting that life is finite can actually reduce worry, because it reminds us our hardships won't last forever. When we recognize our limited time, we tend to focus on what's truly important—like close relationships and simple joys—which naturally brings calm and contentment. Instead of dreading the future, we learn to find gratitude in the present, easing anxiety and opening the door to genuine happiness.

Chapter 3 - Facing Mortality: Fears and Uncertainties

How does reflecting on death spur personal growth?

Reflecting on death can highlight what truly matters, prompting us to be more intentional with our choices. Knowing our time is limited often inspires us to pursue meaningful goals, invest in deeper relationships, and drop minor resentments. In this way, awareness of mortality becomes a catalyst for self-improvement, guiding us to live with greater purpose and to care more deeply for others.

Chapter 3 - Facing Mortality: Fears and Uncertainties

Does mortality give life more meaning?

Yes. Recognizing that our days are numbered adds urgency and depth to how we live, pushing us to focus on genuine priorities like love, connection, and service. Each moment feels more significant when we understand it's fleeting, and this heightened appreciation can bring a greater sense of purpose. By seeing everyone share the same ultimate destiny, we foster empathy and choose experiences that truly enrich our lives, making every day more meaningful.

Chapter 3 - Facing Mortality: Fears and Uncertainties

Why is death a difficult topic to discuss?

Talking about death can feel uncomfortable because it forces us to confront our own mortality, unresolved emotions, and uncertain outcomes. Cultural taboos often discourage open conversations, leaving death shrouded in silence. Yet discussing it can be profoundly healing, helping us process fear, guilt, and the reality of impermanence.

Far from being morbid, these candid exchanges deepen our appreciation for life and strengthen our connections. By acknowledging our shared fate, we not only address lingering anxieties but also find renewed purpose in the time we have. Ultimately, facing the topic of death can guide us to live more fully, with gratitude and intention.

Chapter 3 - Facing Mortality: Fears and Uncertainties

Are we all truly equal in death?

Yes. Death is the ultimate leveler, dissolving all external distinctions such as wealth, status, race, and nationality. Despite our differences in life, we share the same unavoidable fate, which can foster humility and empathy. Recognizing this universal truth reminds us that no one is exempt from life's final moment, and that the material privileges we often cling to ultimately hold no power over our mortality.

What endures beyond death is the impact of our character rather than our worldly achievements. Material possessions cannot follow us; instead, the love we've shown, the kindness we've offered, and the relationships we've nurtured define our lasting legacy. In this sense, death underscores our common humanity and invites us to focus on what truly matters—living with purpose, compassion, and integrity until we, too, reach that shared destination.

Chapter 3 - Facing Mortality: Fears and Uncertainties

Are animals aware of mortality?

We don't know with absolute certainty. While certain species—such as elephants and primates—show behaviors that resemble mourning or cautious avoidance of lethal threats, we lack direct insight into their inner experiences. Elephants, for example, have been observed touching and examining the bones of their deceased companions, hinting at a possible awareness of death. However, these actions might just as easily be learned responses or expressions of social bonding.

Ultimately, we cannot say for sure that animals comprehend mortality in the way humans do. Their instincts and social behaviors may be sophisticated, but whether they recognize death as a final, universal reality remains speculative. Without the ability to communicate on a deeper cognitive level, much about animals' perceptions of life and death remains a mystery.

CHAPTER 4
The Afterlife and Belief

Questions answered in this chapter:

Can we know what happens after death?

Do we all go to heaven?

What if I worry my sins won't be forgiven before I die?

What if someone doesn't believe in an afterlife?

Will we be reunited with loved ones after death?

Is there a chance for learning or growth in the afterlife?

Is eternal life endless bliss or endless suffering?

Chapter 4 - The Afterlife and Belief

Can we know what happens after death?

On our own, we cannot know for certain what lies beyond, as no one can die and come back to share the details. The afterlife is beyond human experience and scientific observation. The only way we gain reliable knowledge about it is through the information revealed by the All-Knowing Creator, rather than personal testimonies or experiments in this world.

According to that divine revelation, life does not end with death. Instead, each soul faces divine justice, where its choices, intentions, and deeds are weighed. Those who have lived righteously receive rewards, while those who have turned away face the consequences of their actions. In this sense, death marks not a final exit but the beginning of a higher reality where every soul is treated with perfect fairness.

Chapter 4 - The Afterlife and Belief

Do we all go to heaven?

No, not everyone is guaranteed entry into heaven. Each person is held accountable for their actions and intentions, and heaven is the eternal reward for those who sincerely strive for righteousness. Every deed—good or bad—is taken into account, ensuring that no effort is overlooked and no wrong goes unaddressed.

Those who persist in wrongdoing face consequences that reflect the Creator's justice and mercy. In the end, the Creator's perfect wisdom governs each soul's eternal outcome, making certain that every individual is treated with absolute fairness.

Chapter 4 - The Afterlife and Belief

What if I worry my sins won't be forgiven before I die?

It's natural to worry about past wrongdoings, especially when thinking about the finality of death. The path to peace begins with sincere repentance: honestly acknowledging your sins, seeking forgiveness, and making amends where possible. True repentance involves a commitment to living righteously from this point forward.

The Creator's mercy is vast, offering hope to anyone who sincerely turns to Him. As long as you are alive, there remains a chance for forgiveness and renewal. Instead of feeling trapped by guilt and fear, trust in the compassion and justice of the One who knows your intentions and your efforts to change.

Chapter 4 - The Afterlife and Belief

What if someone doesn't believe in an afterlife?

Personal belief does not change the reality of what follows death. The afterlife is a universal truth that applies to every soul—whether that soul acknowledges it or denies it. Throughout history and across cultures, many have found guidance and accountability in the conviction that our earthly life is merely a stage in a greater journey.

For those who reject the idea of an afterlife, attention may shift entirely to worldly priorities. Yet unbelief does not negate the inevitability of death or what lies beyond. Ultimately, the afterlife is not a matter of personal preference but a shared destiny each of us will encounter in due course.

Chapter 4 - The Afterlife and Belief

Will we be reunited with loved ones after death?

Yes. In many cases, we will be reunited with the people we love, though the afterlife does not simply replicate our earthly bonds. Guided by divine justice and mercy, those who persist in wrongdoing may not reside alongside those who pursued righteousness. While our relationships here do matter, spiritual realities ultimately shape how we connect in the hereafter.

Even so, love and goodness do not end when we die. The kindness, faith, and compassion we show in this life carry over and influence our eternal relationships. In the end, the Creator's perfect wisdom balances justice and mercy, ensuring that each soul's eternal home reflects the life it led.

Chapter 4 - The Afterlife and Belief

Is there a chance for learning or growth in the afterlife?

Perspectives differ widely. Some believe that once we die, the afterlife simply reflects the outcomes of our earthly choices, leaving little scope for further development or change. Others hold that the soul continues to learn, evolving in a realm that deepens its spiritual connection. In either view, most agree that how we live now—our deeds, intentions, and devotion—directly shapes our eternal condition.

While the specifics vary from one belief system to another, the common thread is that our time in this world matters greatly. Whether the afterlife offers growth or primarily enacts final results, our present actions have lasting significance. Ultimately, living with integrity and purpose here lays the foundation for whatever comes next.

Chapter 4 - The Afterlife and Belief

Is eternal life endless bliss or endless suffering?

Eternal life can offer boundless joy or perpetual hardship, depending on the state of the soul. A soul that pursues goodness and righteousness experiences eternal bliss, while one burdened by persistent wrongdoing or separation from virtue may face enduring suffering.

In this realm of perfect justice, each soul reaps what it has sown through its deeds and intentions. No act of kindness goes unrewarded, and no wrongdoing is overlooked. In that sense, eternal life reflects the natural consequences of how one has lived, allowing every individual to encounter the outcome they have ultimately earned.

Chapter 5

Contact with the Deceased: Myths and Realities

Questions answered in this chapter:

Does a deceased person see or hear us?

Can the deceased help or influence events in this life?

Can a deceased person intercede for me?

Is it permissible to pray to the deceased?

Do spirits or 'energies' linger in familiar places?

Is it okay to think about someone who died?

Can I keep a relationship with someone who died?

Do dreams about the deceased mean anything?

Chapter 5 - Contact with the Deceased: Myths and Realities

Does a deceased person see or hear us?

When a person dies, their soul departs from the body, which no longer functions the same way. Sight, hearing, and other earthly abilities do not operate as they once did. The soul moves into a different realm, beyond our usual perception and physical laws.

Because of this separation, those who have passed on are no longer capable of observing or listening to us in the way they did during life. Their awareness now follows spiritual realities, free from earthly senses. While we may still feel their presence through memories and influence, it differs from having a tangible, ongoing connection or any ordinary means of communication.

Chapter 5 - Contact with the Deceased: Myths and Realities

Can the deceased help or influence events in this life?

No. After death, the soul departs from the physical world and can no longer act upon it. Any influence the deceased may have is carried on through the values, memories, and lessons they leave behind, rather than through direct intervention in our present affairs.

True support ultimately comes from the Creator, as well as the living community around us. While the legacy of those who have passed can inspire us and shape our decisions, we should not expect them to guide or alter current events. Our reliance remains on divine help and on those who share this life with us.

Chapter 5 - Contact with the Deceased: Myths and Realities

Can a deceased person intercede for me?

Intercession—appealing to the Creator on someone's behalf—ultimately depends on the Creator's will. Some teachings hold that prophets or deeply pious individuals may be granted permission to intercede for others, even after their death. However, this privilege is never under human control; it remains subject to the Creator's boundless justice and mercy.

No one can override the Creator's perfect wisdom. While the possibility of intercession can offer hope, it does not absolve us of personal responsibility. Our deeds, intentions, and direct relationship with the Creator carry profound weight in determining our ultimate outcome.

Chapter 5 - Contact with the Deceased: Myths and Realities

Is it permissible to pray to the deceased?

No. We should pray for the deceased—asking the Creator to grant them mercy, forgiveness, and peace—rather than praying to them. Once a person has passed away, they can no longer see, hear, or act in this world. True help and blessings come only from the Creator, who governs all affairs. While it's natural to feel a continued bond with loved ones who have passed, any plea for intervention should be directed to the One who holds ultimate authority.

In honoring those who have departed, we preserve their memory by praying on their behalf and upholding the good they left behind. This reflects our love for them while recognizing that they now exist in a realm beyond direct communication. By directing our prayers to the Creator, we demonstrate proper reverence and trust in the only One who can truly grant help, mercy, and guidance.

Chapter 5 - Contact with the Deceased: Myths and Realities

Do spirits or 'energies' linger in familiar places?

Although some traditions describe restless spirits or subtle energies remaining in places once inhabited by the deceased, many beliefs affirm that when the soul departs, it moves on to a separate realm. Any perceived "presence" is often rooted in our own memories and emotional bonds rather than an actual lingering spirit.

This attachment to familiar spaces and objects is natural, reflecting our desire to stay connected to loved ones. However, once someone has truly passed on, their active influence in this world ceases. Cherishing memories is a healthy way to honor their legacy, but it's important to recognize that the departed have moved beyond the realm of earthly interactions.

Chapter 5 - Contact with the Deceased: Myths and Realities

Is it okay to think about someone who died?

Yes. It's both natural and healthy to reflect on the memories of loved ones who have died. Remembering them can bring us comfort and honor their life, helping us appreciate the love and experiences we shared. By praying for them or recalling their positive qualities and impact, we keep their legacy alive in our hearts.

At the same time, finding the right balance is important. Focusing too much on the past can slow our personal growth and distract us from responsibilities in the present. Healthy reflection means cherishing fond memories of those who have passed without letting them overshadow our current life, allowing us to honor them while still moving forward.

Chapter 5 - Contact with the Deceased: Myths and Realities

Can I keep a relationship with someone who died?

A literal, two-way relationship isn't possible once a person has passed, as they can no longer interact with us from their realm. Still, it's perfectly natural to reflect on a deceased loved one's influence, cherish shared memories, and honor the role they played in your life. Our ultimate spiritual relationship rests with the Creator, who is always present and attentive to our needs.

By recalling the lessons and love they left behind—without seeking direct communication—you keep their memory alive while continuing to move forward. This balanced approach allows you to honor their legacy and acknowledge the growth they inspired, all within the Creator's ongoing care and guidance.

Chapter 5 - Contact with the Deceased: Myths and Realities

Do dreams about the deceased mean anything?

Dreams often mirror our emotional state. Seeing a departed loved one may reflect ongoing grief or a longing to reconnect, offering a way for the mind to process loss. From a psychological standpoint, these dreams can bring unresolved feelings to the surface, while from a spiritual perspective, some see them as reminders of our enduring bond.

Regardless of interpretation, such dreams can provide comfort. However, it's important to keep your focus on the present and maintain a relationship with the Creator, recognizing that your loved one's earthly journey has ended. Acknowledging these dreams without becoming overly fixated on them can help you honor cherished memories while continuing to live fully.

CHAPTER 6
Grief and Emotional Responses

Questions answered in this chapter:

Why do we grieve after someone dies?

Is it normal to cry or feel numb after a loss?

What if I don't cry or feel sad after losing someone?

How do I cope with the death of a loved one?

How can I handle guilt after losing a loved one?

Is it wrong to feel happy after losing someone?

Why do we feel anger after a loss?

What are the stages of grief? Are they universal?

Is my grief normal, or is it depression or mental illness?

How can I heal after parting on bad terms?

Does time heal all wounds? Does grief last forever?

Why do some people avoid grieving?

Chapter 5 - Contact with the Deceased: Myths and Realities

Why are some at peace with death, and others not?

Can someone's death bring relief to those left behind?

How and why do relationships change after a death?

Chapter 6 - Grief and Emotional Responses

Why do we grieve after someone dies?

We grieve because we love, and because the person we've lost was often a foundational pillar in our life. Their absence creates a profound void, leaving us to face a reality that suddenly feels incomplete. Though painful, grief is a healthy and necessary response—one that helps us acknowledge our loss and begin the difficult work of adapting to life without them.

By allowing ourselves to feel sorrow, we honor the significance of who they were and the role they played in our world. In time, this process can remind us to treasure the relationships we still have, moving forward with renewed gratitude and understanding. Through grief, we heal, learn, and eventually rebuild our lives in a way that respects both the past and the future.

Is it normal to cry or feel numb after a loss?

Yes. Some people grieve by crying openly and frequently, while others initially feel numb or detached, especially after a sudden or overwhelming loss. This numbness can act as a temporary emotional buffer, giving you time to process what's happened. There's no single "right" or "wrong" response; everyone experiences grief in their own way.

If persistent numbness becomes worrisome or interferes with your daily life, consider reaching out to a trusted friend, counselor, or support group. Talking about your feelings can help you find clarity and remind you that you're not alone in your journey of healing.

Chapter 6 - Grief and Emotional Responses

What if I don't cry or feel sad after losing someone?

It's more common than you might think to experience a sense of detachment or emotional blankness after a loss. Sometimes, this "numbness" is a protective response, giving your mind and body time to adjust. People also grieve in different ways: not everyone shows sadness outwardly, and the depth of the relationship can shape how grief unfolds. If you didn't share a close bond with the deceased, or if other stressors are at play, you might not feel the sorrow you anticipated.

Delayed grief—emotions surfacing weeks or months later—is also a possibility. Each grief journey is unique, and feeling "nothing" at first doesn't necessarily mean you've processed the loss already. It could be your psyche's way of shielding you until you're ready to face deeper emotions. If you're concerned about ongoing numbness, talking with a counselor or trusted friend may help you understand and navigate these complex feelings.

Chapter 6 - Grief and Emotional Responses

How do I cope with the death of a loved one?

Coping often begins with recognizing and accepting your emotions—whether they take the form of shock, sadness, anger, or disbelief. Allow yourself to feel these responses without judgment and lean on family, friends, or trusted individuals for support. Their presence can bring solace and help you process the initial waves of grief.

Many people find healing through meaningful actions, such as prayer, reflection on cherished memories, or creating keepsakes to honor their loved one's life. It's also important to remember that grief is not linear; it may ebb and flow over time. If the pain becomes overwhelming, consider reaching out to a counselor or joining a support group. You don't have to navigate this journey alone, and the love you shared continues to shape who you are as you move forward.

Chapter 6 - Grief and Emotional Responses

How can I handle guilt after losing a loved one?

It's natural to feel guilt amid grief—perhaps from unspoken words, unresolved conflicts, or even the simple fact that you survived while they did not. Begin by acknowledging your emotions, reflecting on why you feel guilty, and discerning whether that guilt is fully warranted. Seeking forgiveness from the Creator and practicing self-forgiveness can help relieve the burden of regret.

It also helps to share your thoughts, whether with a trusted friend, counselor, spiritual advisor, or through writing in a journal. Expressing these feelings brings clarity and can guide you toward self-compassion. Over time, reflecting on past regrets and transforming them into positive changes in your life can bring a sense of peace, allowing you to honor your loved one's memory while moving forward in a healthier way.

Chapter 6 - Grief and Emotional Responses

Is it wrong to feel happy after losing someone?

No. Rediscovering joy after a loss is a natural part of the healing process, not a betrayal of your loved one's memory. Grief doesn't require us to remain in sorrow forever; finding moments of light and comfort reflects resilience and honors the love you shared.

As you resume everyday activities or discover new reasons to smile, you're not minimizing the significance of your loss. Rather, you're evolving through grief and integrating it into your life. It's possible to carry the memory of a loved one in your heart while still allowing yourself to embrace hope, gratitude, and renewed happiness.

Chapter 6 - Grief and Emotional Responses

Why do we feel anger after a loss?

Anger often arises from feelings of helplessness, frustration, or a sense of injustice. It may be directed at the circumstances, oneself, or even the deceased for "leaving." Some people also feel anger toward the Creator for allowing such a painful event. Though these emotions can be intense, they are a natural part of the grieving process.

Acknowledging and expressing this anger—through open conversation, writing, or prayer—helps release the tension it creates. Over time, acceptance can gradually replace anger, although everyone's path is different. Recognizing that anger is a valid response to loss allows you to process it in a healthier way, ultimately moving toward greater peace and understanding.

Chapter 6 - Grief and Emotional Responses

What are the stages of grief? Are they universal?

The five commonly cited stages—denial, anger, bargaining, depression, and acceptance—provide a widely recognized framework for understanding typical reactions to loss. However, these stages are not universal, nor are they strictly sequential. Many people may skip one or more stages, revisit certain emotions multiple times, or experience them in a different order.

Grief is deeply personal, and shaped by factors such as individual beliefs, relationships, and life experiences. While the five-stage model can help us make sense of our feelings, it's essential to remember that each person's journey unfolds in its own unique way.

Chapter 6 - Grief and Emotional Responses

Is my grief normal, or is it depression or mental illness?

Normal grief often comes in waves—periods of sadness, longing, or even guilt interspersed with moments of calm or the ability to find small pleasures. Over time, the intense feelings typically begin to ease, although they may never disappear entirely. You may still look forward to certain activities or feel brief moments of happiness, even as you continue to mourn.

By contrast, clinical depression or other mental health concerns often involve persistent hopelessness, numbness, or despair. You might lose interest in daily life, struggle to function, or have thoughts of self-harm. If your grief remains overwhelming for several months or disrupts daily tasks, it may be time to seek professional help. A qualified counselor or mental health professional can offer support and hope. There is no shame in asking for assistance when grief becomes unmanageable.

Chapter 6 - Grief and Emotional Responses

How can I heal after parting on bad terms?

It's natural to feel regret or sadness when someone passes away before you can mend a conflict. Begin by acknowledging any guilt, anger, or resentment you may still carry. Practice forgiveness—for both the deceased and yourself—knowing that while you can't change the past, you can ease the burden of unresolved emotions. Reflect on what the conflict taught you and use those lessons to strengthen your relationships going forward.

You might also consider sharing your feelings with a trusted friend, counselor, or spiritual advisor, allowing you to work through emotions in a safe setting. Prayer or compassionate reflection can deepen your trust in the Creator's mercy and wisdom, reminding you that healing is possible even without a face-to-face resolution. In time, self-compassion and acceptance can ease lingering regrets, freeing you to move forward with greater peace and a lighter heart.

Chapter 6 - Grief and Emotional Responses

Does time heal all wounds? Does grief last forever?

Time doesn't always erase grief entirely, but it often softens its intensity. The sharp edge of loss can gradually dull, allowing people to live with a gentler sorrow. Still, waves of sadness may return on anniversaries or when special memories resurface. For most, healing involves integrating the loss into everyday life—finding ways to carry on while cherishing the memory of what was lost.

Though some sadness may linger, it can become a quieter, more reflective reminder of how deeply you loved. This evolving perspective can foster wisdom, empathy, and a renewed appreciation for the gift of life.

Chapter 6 - Grief and Emotional Responses

Why do some people avoid grieving?

Many individuals steer clear of grief because they see it as a sign of weakness, fear its overwhelming intensity, or lack a supportive environment where they can safely express their feelings. In some cultures, open displays of sorrow are discouraged, adding social pressure to remain stoic. Others may even deny the reality of death itself, finding it too painful to accept—this denial can serve as a temporary buffer against overwhelming emotions, but it also postpones the natural process of grieving.

Yet grief is a crucial part of healing. Suppressing sorrow often leads to unresolved emotions that may reappear later in more complicated forms, like anxiety, anger, or depression. By acknowledging and experiencing grief, we ultimately allow ourselves to process the loss and adapt to a new reality. This honest engagement with pain fosters greater emotional resilience and healthier coping methods in the long run.

Chapter 6 - Grief and Emotional Responses

Why are some at peace with death, and others not?

For many, peace comes from acceptance, spiritual grounding, or a sense of having lived a meaningful life. Trusting in a greater plan can foster a calm approach to death, especially when individuals feel they have fulfilled their responsibilities and reconciled any regrets. This readiness often grows out of self-reflection, faith, and the belief that there is more to existence than what we see in this world.

Others struggle with death because of lingering doubts, strong attachments, or uncertainty about what lies beyond. Anxiety may arise from guilt over past actions or the reluctance to leave loved ones behind. In these cases, fear can overshadow the possibility of peace. Ultimately, coming to terms with death—emotionally and spiritually—helps transform it from a source of dread into a natural part of life's journey.

Chapter 6 - Grief and Emotional Responses

Can someone's death bring relief to those left behind?

Yes, it can. When death concludes a long period of suffering or ends a deeply stressful situation, loved ones may experience relief alongside their sorrow. This reaction doesn't indicate a lack of love; rather, it recognizes that a heavy burden has been lifted—whether the burden belonged to the deceased or those who cared for them. In some cases, relief may even stem from the end of a strained relationship.

Acknowledging these conflicting emotions is key to processing grief in a healthy way. Recognizing that sadness, relief, and even guilt can coexist helps prevent unresolved feelings from lingering. By allowing space for these complex responses, individuals can better honor the totality of their experience and move forward with greater emotional clarity.

Chapter 6 - Grief and Emotional Responses

How and why do relationships change after a death?

Death can reshape roles and emotional bonds, sometimes drawing people closer through shared grief, while in other cases creating distance if they cope in conflicting ways. The loss of a central figure may require significant adjustments, altering routines, and redefining family or friendship dynamics. Emotions like guilt, regret, or a heightened sense of appreciation can lead to new priorities and perspectives.

As a result, some relationships deepen through mutual support, while others naturally fade as life paths diverge. Patience, empathy, and open communication are key to navigating these shifts. By acknowledging and accommodating each other's needs, loved ones can help one another find balance and understanding in the wake of loss.

CHAPTER 7
Faith, Doubt, and Spiritual Perspectives

Questions answered in this chapter:

Does faith change our perception of death?

Is it normal to question my faith after a major loss?

Is anger toward the Creator normal after a major loss?

Do all religions view death the same way?

Is the angel of death real?

What do near-death experiences teach us?

Chapter 7 - Faith, Doubt, and Spiritual Perspectives

Does faith change our perception of death?

Yes. For many people, faith reframes death from an abrupt ending to a passage into a greater reality. Belief in an afterlife or trust in the Higher Power can ease fears, bring comfort, and foster hope. This spiritual perspective often provides clarity about life's purpose, helping individuals accept mortality with greater peace.

For those who do not follow a particular faith, other guiding values or personal philosophies can still influence their view of death. Whether through the hope of a legacy, the strength of relationships, or a commitment to living meaningfully, each person's beliefs shape how they process the final chapter of life. Ultimately, faith—however defined—can offer a path to understanding death that aligns with one's deepest convictions and experiences.

Chapter 7 - Faith, Doubt, and Spiritual Perspectives

Is it normal to question my faith after a major loss?

Yes. Grief can disrupt your sense of certainty, leading you to ask why this happened and whether there is a greater purpose or plan. In the wake of deep sorrow, it's not unusual to wonder if the beliefs you held still provide comfort or answers. This questioning often arises because a major loss magnifies life's fragility, putting the reality of pain and suffering front and center.

Over time, acknowledging these doubts can foster a deeper, more resilient faith. Wrestling with hard questions can prompt you to re-examine what you believe and why, potentially strengthening your understanding of the Creator's design. Instead of weakening your faith, honest reflection can lead to a more profound sense of trust and purpose, even as you grapple with sadness.

Is anger toward the Creator normal after a major loss?

Yes. Anger toward the Creator is a common response when a loss feels senseless or unjust. You might wonder why a loving and powerful God would allow such pain, especially if you've prayed for a different outcome. This anger is not a sign of weak faith; rather, it reflects the raw intensity of grief and your desire for life to be fair and predictable.

It's crucial to let yourself feel and express this anger, rather than bottling it up. Confiding in someone you trust—a counselor, spiritual advisor, or empathetic friend—can help you process these emotions. In time, working through anger can lead to deeper spiritual clarity and acceptance, allowing you to reconcile your pain with the Creator's greater design, even if that design remains partially hidden.

Chapter 7 - Faith, Doubt, and Spiritual Perspectives

Do all religions view death the same way?

No. Around the world, different faiths and cultures hold diverse beliefs about what happens when life ends. Some teach the existence of heaven and hell, others describe a cycle of rebirth, and some view death as a conclusion. These beliefs often reflect broader perspectives on the nature of the soul, morality, and the ultimate purpose of existence.

Still, death is a universal experience that transcends cultural and religious differences. Exploring various viewpoints can deepen our understanding of life's fragility and highlight the shared human quest for meaning. In facing mortality, people across all traditions grapple with grief, hope, and the desire for comfort—reminding us that, despite differing beliefs, we are united by our need to make sense of life's inevitable end.

Chapter 7 - Faith, Doubt, and Spiritual Perspectives

Is the angel of death real?

Yes. The angel of death is a being appointed by the Creator to take each soul at its designated time. Unlike the grim figure depicted in stories, this angel operates under divine command, ensuring that every life concludes according to the Creator's perfect measure.

How the angel appears depends on the soul's spiritual condition. For someone who lived with faith in the Creator and followed a righteous path, its arrival is gentle. For one who persisted in wrongdoing, the experience is harsher. In both cases, the angel simply fulfills the Creator's will, reflecting justice, mercy, and wisdom.

Chapter 7 - Faith, Doubt, and Spiritual Perspectives

What do near-death experiences teach us?

Near-death experiences (NDEs) happen when people come close to dying yet survive, often reporting vivid sensations or an overwhelming sense of peace. While profoundly transformative, NDEs differ from true death because the body and brain still function at some level. Those who describe these events frequently speak of tunnels of light, encounters with spiritual beings, or a detached view of their own bodies.

These experiences can prompt deep reflection on life's fragility, our mind-body-spirit connection, and the possibility of realities beyond our current understanding. Whether approached from a scientific or spiritual perspective, NDEs often spark renewed gratitude, empathy, and intentional living—reminding us that the boundary between life and what lies beyond may be more mysterious than we realize.

CHAPTER 8
Complex End-of-Life Questions

Questions answered in this chapter:

Is it natural to wish for death during hard times?

Is it ever justifiable to end one's own life?

What is euthanasia, and why is it controversial?

Should we use all medical means to prolong life?

Can someone return to life after dying?

Can someone bring the dead back to life?

Chapter 8 - Complex End-of-Life Questions

Is it natural to wish for death during hard times?

Yes. In moments of deep despair, loneliness, or overwhelming stress, it's not uncommon for people to feel they can't go on. Wishing for death can be a sign of intense emotional pain rather than a firm, unchangeable desire to die. It often reflects a temporary state of mind—an urgent signal that support or intervention is needed.

Reaching out to others can bring relief and a renewed sense of hope. Confiding in trusted friends, seeking professional help, or talking with a spiritual advisor can help you regain perspective and discover healthier ways to cope. Even the darkest moments may serve as turning points for personal growth when met with understanding and compassion. If you or someone you know feels this way, remember that help is available and brighter days may lie ahead.

Chapter 8 - Complex End-of-Life Questions

Is it ever justifiable to end one's own life?

No. Life is a sacred trust from the Creator, meant to last until its natural conclusion. Though hardships can at times feel overwhelming, they also present opportunities to grow, build resilience, and discover new solutions. Even in the darkest moments, hope and meaning remain within reach, reminding us that pain, while real, does not have to be permanent.

If you or someone you know is grappling with despair, seeking professional help and turning to supportive friends or community members are crucial steps. With the right guidance and care, many people rediscover a sense of hope and resolution—realizing that life still holds promise beyond their current struggles. Ultimately, no matter how bleak the situation appears, there is potential for renewal and the resolution of even life's toughest challenges.

Chapter 8 - Complex End-of-Life Questions

What is euthanasia, and why is it controversial?

Euthanasia—often called "mercy killing"—is the act of intentionally ending someone's life to relieve suffering. Advocates view it as a compassionate choice that respects personal autonomy, particularly in cases of terminal illness or unmanageable pain. Opponents, however, see it as undermining the sanctity of life, arguing that only the Creator can determine when life should end. Opponents also express worries about potential abuses and whether society might begin to undervalue human life if euthanasia becomes acceptable.

Because of these moral, cultural, and spiritual concerns, many countries place strict limits on or outright ban euthanasia. The debate ultimately hinges on how we balance an individual's desire to end suffering against a broader commitment to preserving life, reflecting the complex values societies hold around autonomy, compassion, and the nature of death.

Chapter 8 - Complex End-of-Life Questions

Should we use all medical means to prolong life?

Life is indeed precious, and many believe we have a duty to preserve it whenever possible. However, there comes a point where additional procedures may only extend suffering rather than improve quality of life. In those situations, shifting to palliative or comfort care can respect life's sanctity while also acknowledging its natural limits.

Ultimately, each case is unique and merits thoughtful consideration. By seeking medical counsel, spiritual guidance, and input from loved ones, individuals can make decisions that honor both the value of life and the reality that no one is meant to remain in this world indefinitely. This balanced approach upholds the dignity of the patient while entrusting life's final outcome to the Creator's Wisdom.

Chapter 8 - Complex End-of-Life Questions

Can someone return to life after dying?

No. Once a person truly dies—meaning the soul has departed the body—there is no returning to worldly life. What we sometimes call "clinical death" involves a momentary shutdown of vital functions while the soul remains present, allowing modern medicine to restart the heart or support failing organs. This temporary state differs from actual, irreversible death.

According to this understanding, the soul's separation from the body marks the end of life in this world. Any future return to life will occur only on the day of resurrection, by the Creator's command—a realm of divine authority beyond human power or intervention.

Chapter 8 - Complex End-of-Life Questions

Can someone bring the dead back to life?

No. Restoring true life to someone who has completely passed away—meaning their soul has left the body—is beyond human power. Medical interventions can sometimes revive those who are near death or in a temporary state of "clinical death," but that differs from resurrecting someone whose life has truly ended.

This distinction underscores our human limitations and points to the Creator's ultimate authority over life and death. While science can help sustain or restart basic bodily functions in certain cases, it cannot return a departed soul to the body once genuine death has occurred.

CHAPTER 9
Overcoming Fear and Living Fully

Questions answered in this chapter:

How can I stop worrying about death?

How do I find peace with death?

How can I live fully knowing I will die?

Chapter 9 - Overcoming Fear and Living Fully

How can I stop worrying about death?

It's natural to feel uneasy about death, especially when we cannot control or fully understand it. Instead of letting fear consume you, consider viewing death as a natural part of life's design. Preparing yourself—spiritually, emotionally, and even practically—can transform anxiety into a sense of peace. Reflecting on your beliefs about life, and trusting in the Creator's Wisdom, helps ground you in the idea that death is inevitable yet purposeful.

At the same time, remember that your present moments remain yours to shape. Focusing on what you can control—like nurturing relationships, pursuing meaningful goals, and taking care of your well-being—can reduce the weight of these worries. By accepting death as a shared destiny, you free up energy to live more deeply in the here and now.

Chapter 9 - Overcoming Fear and Living Fully

How do I find peace with death?

Reflecting on death can bring clarity, prompting us to let go of trivial concerns and invest in deeper, more meaningful relationships. By recognizing our limited time, we often gain a renewed focus on what truly matters, whether it's spiritual growth, genuine connections, or acts of service. This perspective turns mortality from a source of dread into a motivating force for living with greater purpose and compassion.

Seeing life and death as interconnected parts of a divine plan can also provide comfort. It reassures us that our brief existence here contributes to something much larger and more enduring. Rather than viewing death as an abrupt end, it becomes part of a continuous story—one in which our actions, values, and relationships hold lasting significance.

Chapter 9 - Overcoming Fear and Living Fully

How can I live fully knowing I will die?

Recognizing life's brevity can bring a sense of urgency and clarity. Rather than fearing death, let it serve as a reminder of life's value and the importance of each moment. Focus on what truly matters—nurturing relationships, pursuing passions, and extending kindness to others. By savoring each day and being present, you enrich your experiences and deepen your connections.

Living fully also means transforming the inevitability of death into motivation for gratitude, personal growth, and meaningful impact. Use the reality of your limited time to prioritize what counts, embracing the opportunities you have now. In doing so, you cultivate a life marked by purpose, warmth, and a deep appreciation for every precious moment.

Chapter 10
Children and Death

Questions answered in this chapter:

Why do some people die young?

How do children see death differently than adults?

How do I help a child understand death?

How do I help a child cope with losing a loved one?

Chapter 10 - Children and Death

Why do some people die young?

Losing someone at a young age can seem profoundly unfair and often brings deep pain and confusion. Yet each life, no matter how brief, has profound worth and fulfills a specific purpose in the Creator's plan. While we may not fully understand the reasons, their allotted time is neither accidental nor meaningless.

A short life can still resonate deeply, reminding us to cherish our moments and loved ones. Even in its brevity, such a life can leave a lasting imprint on hearts and minds, ultimately pointing us toward greater gratitude, compassion, and trust in a plan beyond our understanding.

Chapter 10 - Children and Death

How do children see death differently than adults?

Children's grasp of death evolves in stages. Younger children may view death as temporary or reversible, shaped by imagination or media depictions. They might ask the same questions repeatedly or blend fantasy and reality. As children grow older, they begin to understand the permanence of death but often focus on practical details—like what happens to the body—more than the emotional or spiritual aspects that adults might emphasize.

Additionally, children tend to grieve in short bursts, dipping into moments of deep sadness but then returning to normal play or activities. Their emotional responses can appear inconsistent or confusing from an adult's perspective. Recognizing these developmental differences allows parents and caregivers to provide patient, age-appropriate support, ensuring that children feel safe to ask questions, share their feelings, and gradually integrate the concept of loss.

Chapter 10 - Children and Death

How do I help a child understand death?

Start with simple, clear language that matches their age and developmental level. Avoid euphemisms like "gone to sleep," as they can create confusion or unnecessary fears. Instead, explain that when a person or animal dies, their body stops working—they don't breathe, eat, or feel pain anymore. Invite the child to ask questions, and answer as honestly as you can, using words they'll understand.

It's also important to acknowledge their emotions. Reassure them that it's perfectly normal to feel sad, curious, or worried. Encourage them to share their thoughts, and remind them that they can keep memories of their loved one alive through stories, photos, or drawings. By creating a safe space for open conversation, you give the child a chance to process death in a healthy, age-appropriate way.

Chapter 10 - Children and Death

How do I help a child cope with losing a loved one?

Create a safe environment where the child can express their feelings—whether through talking, drawing, or playing. Reassure them that sadness and tears are natural responses to loss. It also helps to keep daily routines as consistent as possible, providing stability during a time of uncertainty. If the child continues to struggle, consider seeking professional help.

Above all, let them know they are not alone in their grief. Offer steady love, understanding, and patience, and be available to listen whenever they want to talk. Your consistent presence and empathy can make a significant difference in helping a child cope and eventually heal from loss.

CHAPTER 11
Supporting Others Through Death

Questions answered in this chapter:

How can I comfort someone who is grieving?

How can I support someone who is dying?

Chapter 11 - Supporting Others Through Death

How can I comfort someone who is grieving?

Begin by offering a compassionate, nonjudgmental presence. Listen actively, allowing them to share their emotions without trying to "fix" or minimize their pain. Often, simple, heartfelt words—or even silent support—mean more than well-intentioned clichés. Practical help, such as cooking a meal or running errands, can also lift some of their daily burdens, easing the pressure they feel.

Be patient, understanding that grief ebbs and flows at its own pace. Avoid rushing their healing or suggesting they "move on." Instead, let them know they're not alone in their sorrow. Your steady presence can provide reassurance and comfort as they navigate this difficult chapter of their life.

Chapter 11 - Supporting Others Through Death

How can I support someone who is dying?

Supporting a dying person begins with empathy, attentiveness, and understanding. Offer a calm, nonjudgmental presence, allowing them to express their thoughts and emotions, including fears or regrets. Reassure them that it's natural to feel afraid, and if appropriate, provide spiritual support through prayers or quiet reflection. Simple actions like holding their hand, sharing comforting memories, or helping with everyday tasks can bring both practical and emotional relief.

Above all, let them know they are not alone. Listening without trying to solve their problems and affirming their worth can help them feel more at peace in this final stage of life. Your attentive presence and compassionate care remind them that, despite life's fragility, they are loved and supported until the very end.

Chapter 12
Preparing for Our Own End

Questions answered in this chapter:

How do I settle unresolved conflicts before I die?

How do I ensure my dependents' care after I'm gone?

What does it mean to embrace mortality?

Does the world change when we die?

What do we leave behind after we die?

How should we die?

Chapter 12 - Preparing for Our Own End

How do I settle unresolved conflicts before I die?

Begin by identifying the relationships or situations that weigh on your heart. Reflect on your own actions or words, and when possible, offer sincere apologies or extend genuine forgiveness. If a direct resolution isn't feasible, seek closure through personal means—such as writing a letter you won't send, praying, meditating, or confiding in a trusted friend, counselor, or spiritual advisor.

Allowing yourself to move beyond hurt, guilt, or resentment opens the path to greater clarity and peace of mind. By acknowledging what cannot be changed and taking responsibility for your part, you create the emotional space needed to approach life—and the end of life—with compassion, understanding, and inner calm.

Chapter 12 - Preparing for Our Own End

How do I ensure my dependents' care after I'm gone?

Begin with practical preparations such as financial planning, creating a clear will, and designating guardians or caregivers. Openly communicate your wishes so loved ones understand how you want your dependents cared for. By putting these measures in place, you offer a sense of security and stability for those who will remain.

Beyond these tangible efforts, entrusting your dependents to the care of the Supreme Being can bring peace of mind. While we do our best to protect those we love, their ultimate future rests in divine hands. Balancing sound preparation with genuine faith ensures you leave behind both practical support and a profound sense of reassurance for your family.

Chapter 12 - Preparing for Our Own End

What does it mean to embrace mortality?

Embracing mortality means acknowledging that death is a natural part of our human experience. Rather than viewing this fact as grim or unsettling, we use it to sharpen our focus on what matters most—our relationships, our goals, and our moments of genuine joy. By recognizing that our time is limited, we're less likely to waste it on trivial concerns and more likely to treasure everyday wonders, from shared laughter to a peaceful morning walk.

This acceptance doesn't diminish our happiness; instead, it deepens it. When we see life's fragility as a call to be fully present, we invest our energy in building meaningful connections and pursuing goals that give our days real purpose. Embracing mortality, then, isn't about dwelling on death—it's about living with greater intent and gratitude, knowing that every moment carries unique value.

Chapter 12 - Preparing for Our Own End

Does the world change when we die?

Yes, although not always in obvious ways. For those closest to us, our absence can create a profound void—shifting daily routines, roles, and even the emotional landscape within a family or community. People may need time and space to adjust, grieving the loss while learning to navigate life without our presence. In this sense, the immediate world we leave behind does change, sometimes significantly, for those who cared for us.

On a larger scale, the world keeps moving, yet it's subtly reshaped by the legacy each of us leaves behind—our words, deeds, and the values we passed on. Every life adds something unique to the human story, creating ripples that continue long after we're gone. The influence we've had—big or small—remains woven into the fabric of the communities and individuals we touched.

Chapter 12 - Preparing for Our Own End

What do we leave behind after we die?

We leave behind our reputation—defined by both the good and the bad deeds we performed—and the bonds we formed throughout our lives. Our interactions and the love we shared become cherished memories, living on in the stories people tell and the lessons they carry forward. Even our material possessions, though they may pass on to others, are secondary to the intangible legacy we create through our character, kindness, and everyday choices.

Ultimately, the most enduring impact lies in how we have touched the hearts of those around us. Whether through acts of service, simple moments of compassion, or wisdom passed down, our influence shapes the lives we leave behind. Long after we are gone, the ripples of our presence continue to guide and inspire those who remember us.

Chapter 12 - Preparing for Our Own End

How should we die?

We should strive to meet our end in submission to our Creator—at peace with our actions, our purpose, and His plan. This involves living with integrity and gratitude, working to mend broken relationships, reflecting on our choices, and trusting in the Creator's Wisdom. Though we cannot predict the time or circumstances of our passing, faith in His grace allows us to face death with hope and readiness, confident that our final moments are part of a greater design.

The End
Is Not the End

www.ingramcontent.com/pod-product-compliance
Lightning Source LLC
Chambersburg PA
CBHW072057290426
44110CB00014B/1714